Essential Question
Where do good ideas come from?

Clever Puss

by Yvonne Morrin
illustrated by Kieran Rynhart

Chapter 1
Puss Wants Boots 2

Chapter 2
The Contest 6

Chapter 3
A New King 11

Respond to Reading 16

PAIRED READ Rabbit and the Well 17

Focus on Genre 20

Chapter 1
Puss Wants Boots

Once three brothers lived with their father and his cat. The father adored his cat. One day, the father said, "You're all grown now. I'm going on a **journey**. I have gifts for you."

The father gave the two older sons bags of money.

The father turned to his youngest son. "Tom, I am giving you my greatest treasure. You can have Puss!"

He gave the cat to Tom and said good-bye to his sons.

The next day, Tom's brothers went off to spend their money. Tom was alone with the cat.

"You are no use to me, Puss!" cried Tom.

Puss said, "I made your father rich. I can make you **wealthy**, too. If you get me a pair of boots, I'll show you how I can help you."

Tom got a tiny pair of boots for the cat. Puss was very happy with his boots.

Weeks went by and nothing happened. Soon the food began to run out. Tom had no money to buy more.

"Puss, when are you going to make me rich?" Tom whined. "I'm tired of eating old, **stale** food."

The cat smiled.

"You need to go!" Tom shouted.

STOP AND CHECK

What is Tom's problem in the story?

Chapter 2
The Contest

Tom opened the door to put out the cat. There was a letter on the porch. Tom and Puss read it together.

It said the king was holding an **official** contest to find the strongest and speediest citizen. The winner would become king.

"You must enter the contest," Puss told Tom.

"But I'm not strong or speedy!" Tom replied.

"I will **brainstorm** and make a plan," Puss said. "You will win if you listen to me."

The next day, Tom and Puss went to the palace for the contest. There were three other **contestants**. They looked strong and speedy.

The king announced the first contest. "You will throw a ball into the air. You must count to ten before it hits the ground," he said.

The first contestant counted to eight before her ball landed. The next counted to nine. The third person managed to count to ten before his ball hit the ground.

"I won't make it to six," Tom **muttered**. Puss whispered a trick to him.

Tom threw his ball into the air. "Two, four, six, eight, TEN!" he cried before the ball landed.

The king clapped loudly. "What a clever way to count!" he said. The king said that Tom and the third contestant had made it to the next part of the contest. The other two contestants looked **astonished**.

> **STOP AND CHECK**
>
> How does Tom win the first contest?

Chapter 3
A New King

The next contest was a race around the palace. "You must carry a full bag on your back," the king said. "The first contestant to get to the finish line will be the new king."

Puss checked out the bags and the racetrack. He whispered in Tom's ear.

The other contestant chose a light bag that was full of sponges. Tom chose a heavy bag that was full of salt.

"Go!" shouted the king.

The other contestant was ahead of Tom. They came to a river. The other man jumped in and swam **frantically**. The sponges in his bag filled with water. His bag was now very heavy. The other man slowed down.

When Tom jumped in the river, the salt in his bag dissolved in the water and disappeared. The **load** in his bag became very light. Tom won the race.

> **STOP AND CHECK**
>
> What idea helped Tom to win the race?

The king told Tom he was the winner.

"Great!" Tom cried. "When I am king, I can get rid of that cat!"

He turned to Puss. "I don't need your **services** anymore," he said.

Puss said nothing, but his ears **flattened** in anger.

The king frowned at Tom. "You may have won, but Clever Puss gave you the **original** ideas. He whispered in your ear. A king must be **gracious** like Puss. You are a bad winner. Now Puss will be the new king!"

Clever Puss moved into the palace. He was a gracious king. He even **offered** Tom a job. Now Tom cleans Puss's royal boots!

STOP AND CHECK

Why does Clever Puss become the new king?

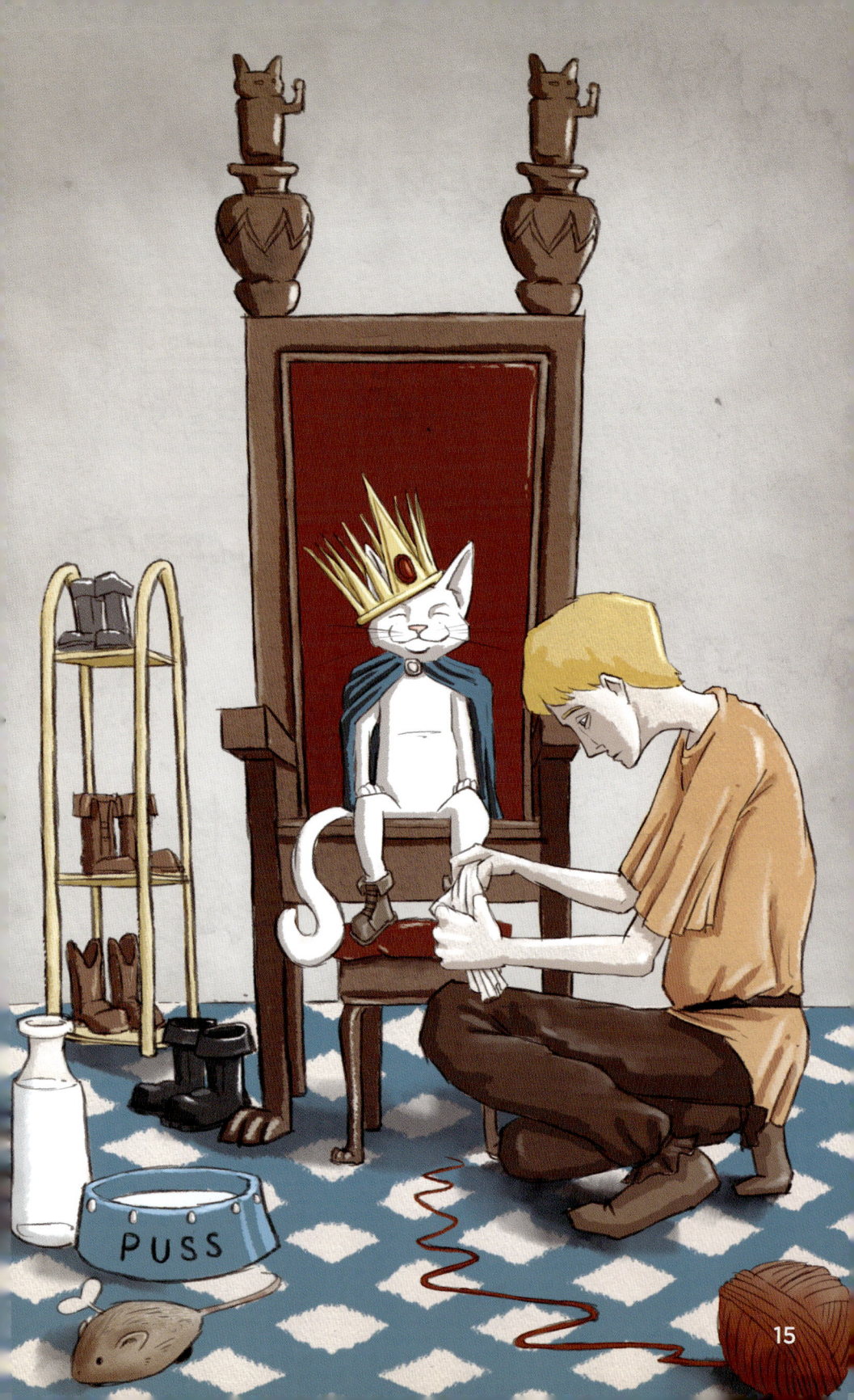

Summarize

Use important details from the story to summarize *Clever Puss*. Your graphic organizer may help you.

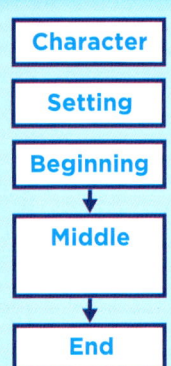

Text Evidence

1. What events led to Puss staying with Tom? **SEQUENCE**

2. Find the word *whined* on page 5. What does it mean? What clues help you figure it out? **VOCABULARY**

3. Write about the events that led to Tom entering the contest. **WRITE ABOUT READING**

Genre Folktale

Compare Texts
Read about how Rabbit tricked Fox.

Rabbit and the Well

Rabbit and Fox were weeding the garden. Rabbit wanted to take a nap, but he didn't want Fox to think he was lazy. Then he had an idea.

"Ouch! I have a thorn in my paw," Rabbit cried. He quickly limped away.

Fox looked at Rabbit suspiciously. Rabbit was up to something.

Rabbit walked past a well. He saw a bucket hanging at the top of the well. "This is a good place for a nap," he said.

He hopped into the bucket. The bucket went down the well and another bucket came up. Rabbit was stuck at the bottom!

Rabbit decided to take his nap at the bottom of the well. Later he heard Fox calling him. "I'm in the well," Rabbit shouted.

Fox looked into the well. "What are you doing?" he asked.

"Fishing," said Rabbit slyly. "Come down."

Fox was hungry. He jumped into the empty bucket. He went down to the bottom of the well. Rabbit went up to the top!

"Happy fishing!" Rabbit called to Fox. Then he hopped away for his nap. He knew that Fox wouldn't interrupt him now.

Make Connections

How did Rabbit trick Fox? **ESSENTIAL QUESTION**

How is Rabbit in *Rabbit and the Well* the same as Puss in *Clever Puss*? How is he different? **TEXT TO TEXT**

Focus on Genre

Fairy Tales Fairy tales have made-up settings and characters. They usually take place long ago. They sometimes include talking animals. Authors sometimes write new versions of fairy tales.

Read and Find *Clever Puss* is a new version of a fairy tale. The story takes place long ago. One of the characters is a talking cat.

Your Turn

Choose an old fairy tale that you know. Change the setting and characters to make them happen today. Make a chart with two columns. List the main features of the old fairy tale in one column. In the other column, list how you used these features in your new fairy tale. Share your chart with a classmate.

Old Fairy Tale	New Fairy Tale